Walk It Out

A 5-Phase Devotional Healing Workbook

BECAUSE HEALING ISN'T LINEAR...
BUT YOUR LIGHT STILL SHINES IN EVERY PHASE.

Marie-Renée

DEDICATION

To every woman brave enough to choose healing over hiding, and to walk out her freedom one step at a time.

To my sisters who refuse to settle for surviving when they were created to thrive.

To those who dare to believe that their wholeness is worth the work.

This is your invitation to walk it out.

BEFORE YOU BEGIN

You hold in your hands more than just a workbook; you hold a practical tool designed to help you walk in the freedom that has already been purchased for you through the blood of Christ. Through five intentional phases, you'll work through exercises, reflections, and truth-based prompts that can help you begin to live out the healing and wholeness that is already yours.

Just like the moon, your healing journey has phases, moments of fullness, renewal, shadow, and growth. But even in the darkest phase, the moon never stops shining. Its light remains, even when it's partially hidden from view. And so it is with you.

There is a light inside of you, a light placed there by your Creator, that never stops illuminating. As you process and progress through the phases of healing, your internal light continues to shine... beautifully, steadily, and faithfully.

This isn't passive reading. This is active engagement with the truth that Christ has already set you free. Each phase contains teaching, reflection, exercises, and planning designed to help you recognize and step into the freedom that is your inheritance as a daughter of God.

What makes this different:

This workbook is based on 18 years of learning to walk out freedom: not theory, but tested practices. Every exercise reflects lessons learned through my real experience about cooperating with God's healing work. You're not getting someone's ideas about healing; you're getting practical tools that have proven helpful in the journey of walking out what Christ has already accomplished.

Fair warning:

This journey will ask hard things of you. You'll face emotions you've avoided, memories you've buried, and patterns you've hidden behind. But as you do this work, you'll discover that God is faithful to meet you in your honesty and help you live out the freedom He's already provided.

You won't approach life the same way at the end of these five phases. The question is: are you ready to begin walking in what's already yours?

Your freedom has already been won

Jesus Christ has already done the work of securing your freedom. This workbook is simply a practical guide to help you learn how to live in that reality. God is already at work. Your job is to show up, engage with the process, and trust Him to help you walk out what He's already accomplished.

Take a deep breath. You're exactly where you need to be.

CONTENTS

HOW TO USE THIS WORKBOOK

This workbook is designed as a 5-phase intensive healing journey, but you control the pace. Each phase contains 2-3 hours of meaningful work including reading, reflection, exercises, and prayer. Some people complete one day per week over five weeks, others take several days to work through each section, and still others spread it over months. Choose what feels sustainable for your life and healing process.

TIME INVESTMENT MATTERS: This isn't casual reading. Each phase requires focused attention and emotional energy. Consider blocking out adequate time when you won't be rushed or interrupted. Many people find it helpful to treat each phase and study time like a personal retreat, setting aside a morning or afternoon to engage fully with the content.

Pacing suggestions:

- If you have 30-60 minutes available: Read the teaching section and begin the reflection questions
- If you have 1-2 hours available: Complete the teaching, reflection, and one exercise section
- If you have 2-3 hours available: Work through an entire phase of content
- If you feel overwhelmed: Take breaks between sections and return when you're ready

Remember: Rushing through defeats the purpose. This work deserves your best attention and intention.

Understanding healing as a process

One of the most important lessons learned through my 18 years of healing journey is this: healing is not a one-time event but an ongoing process. Often, we're in the process of healing long before we recognize it, and we continue healing even when progress feels invisible.

Many people approach healing with an event mindset, expecting a specific moment when everything changes. When that dramatic breakthrough doesn't happen on our timeline, we assume healing isn't occurring. But God's timeline for healing rarely matches our expectations, and His process often works beneath the surface before we see evidence above it.

The truth is, the moment you decided to engage with your healing, the process began. Every honest conversation, every boundary you set, every time you choose vulnerability over hiding: these are healing moments, even if they don't feel transformational in the moment.

This workbook acknowledges healing as a journey with seasons. Some days will feel like breakthrough, others like maintenance, and still others like you're moving backward. All of these are normal parts of the process. Your job isn't to manage the timeline but to show up consistently and trust God's faithfulness in the process.

Each phase contains:

- Scripture & Teaching (2 pages): Core biblical truth and practical insights
- Deep Reflection (2 pages): Questions designed to help you process and understand
- Personal Application (2 pages): Exercises to practice new skills and perspectives
- Assessment & Planning (2 pages): Tools to evaluate progress and plan next steps
- Prayer & Commitment (2 pages): Space to connect with God and commit to action
- Additional Reflection (2 pages): Extra space for continued processing

Essential supplies:

- Quiet space where you won't be interrupted
- Colored pens or pencils for exercises and highlighting
- Tissues (healing can bring tears, and that's okay)
- A comforting, non-alcoholic beverage (tea, coffee, water with lemon)
- Comfortable clothing that helps you feel relaxed and at peace
- An open heart

Working through resistance:

If you find yourself avoiding the workbook, procrastinating, or feeling overwhelmed, that's normal. Resistance often signals you're approaching something important. Remember that healing is happening even when it doesn't feel like it. Sometimes our greatest growth occurs during periods that feel stagnant or difficult. Use the "Difficult Days Toolkit" (page 75) when you need extra support, and trust that God is working even when progress feels invisible.

Getting the most from your journey:

- Be honest in your responses; no one will see this but you
- Don't rush through exercises; let yourself feel and process
- Use the additional reflection space liberally
- Revisit previous days' work as new insights emerge
- Consider sharing your journey with a trusted friend or counselor

After the 5 phases:

Your healing doesn't end when you finish Phase 5. Use the ongoing support tools (pages 73-78) to maintain momentum and continue growing. This workbook is designed to be a resource you return to repeatedly.

Remember:

Healing isn't linear, and it's not confined to dramatic moments of breakthrough. Some days will feel transformational, others will feel like maintenance, and still others might feel challenging. All of these are part of the healing process. Trust that God is working even when progress feels slow or invisible. Often, we're healing long before we recognize it, and growth is happening beneath the surface before we see evidence above it.

YOUR HEALING INTENTION SETTING

Before you begin this journey, take time to clarify your intentions. This isn't about setting goals you can fail at; it's about connecting with your deepest desires for healing and freedom.

Reflection questions:

What brought you to this workbook?

....

....

....

....

What would your life look like if you were completely whole?
Describe your healed self in detail—how you'd feel, act, relate to others, and approach challenges.

....

....

....

....

....

....

What are you most afraid of discovering or facing in this process?

....

....

....

What are you most excited about or hopeful for?

....

....

....

Your Healing Intention Statement: Complete this sentence: "Through this 5-day journey, I am open to God…"

....

....

....

Your Commitment to Yourself: What promise are you making to yourself as you begin this journey?

....

....

....

Date & Signature: Today's Date: _______________

Your Signature: _______________________________

Keep this page accessible. When the journey gets difficult, return here to remember why you started.

PRE-JOURNEY ASSESSMENT

This assessment creates a baseline for your healing journey. Answer honestly—there are no right or wrong responses. You'll return to this assessment after Day 5 to measure your growth.

RATE EACH AREA FROM 1-10: (1 = Significant struggle/pain, 10 = Healthy and whole)

Emotional Health How well do you manage difficult emotions? __/10
Self-Worth How valued and loved do you feel? __/10
Past Trauma How much do past hurts affect your daily life? __/10
Forgiveness (Others) How free are you from resentment and bitterness? __/10
Forgiveness (Self) How kind and patient are you with yourself? __/10
Spiritual Health How connected and close to God do you feel? __/10
Physical Health How well are you caring for your body? __/10
Relationships How healthy and fulfilling are your relationships? __/10
Boundaries How well do you protect your time, energy, and peace? __/10
Life Purpose How clear and passionate are you about your calling? __/10

Your three lowest scores:

These are your priority healing areas for this journey.

1. _______________________ Score: __
2. _______________________ Score: __
3. _______________________ Score: __

Your three highest scores:

These are strengths you can build on.

1. _______________________ Score: __
2. _______________________ Score: __
3. _______________________ Score: __

The one thing:

If God could heal only one thing in your life during these 5 phases, what would you want it to be?

PRAYER & COMMITMENT

A prayer for your journey:

Heavenly Father,

I come to You with my whole heart—the healed parts and the hurting parts. I acknowledge that You are the ultimate Healer, and I invite You into every page of this journey.

Give me courage to face what I've avoided, wisdom to understand what You're teaching me, and faith to believe that healing is not only possible but promised.

Help me be honest about my pain without being overwhelmed by it. Show me how to cooperate with Your healing work without trying to control it.

When I encounter resistance, remind me that breakthrough often comes disguised as difficulty. When I want to quit, remind me that I am worth the work.

Use this workbook to set me free from everything that has held me captive. Transform my pain into purpose, my wounds into wisdom, and my healing into hope for others.

I trust You with my story. I trust You with my heart. I trust You with my healing.

In Jesus' name, amen.

Your personal prayer:

Write your own prayer for this journey:

....

....

....

....

....

....

....

....

....

....

Your commitment:

I commit to approaching this journey with:

- ☐ Honesty about my struggles and pain
- ☐ Openness to what God wants to teach me
- ☐ Patience with the healing process
- ☐ Compassion for myself when it gets difficult
- ☐ Faith that transformation is possible
- ☐ Willingness to do the hard work

Accountability:

Who will you tell about this journey? _______________________

When will you check in with them? _______________________

YOUR SIGNATURE & DATE: _______________________________ Date: ____________

STEP FORWARD IN FAITH

You don't have to feel completely prepared to begin. Sometimes the most important step is the one we take in faith before our emotions catch up. When Jesus told the ten lepers to go show themselves to the priests, Scripture tells us "as they went, they were healed" (Luke 17:14). Their healing came through obedience in motion, not through waiting until they felt ready.

If God has prompted you to engage with this healing journey, trust that He will provide the grace you need as you move forward. Make the faith decision to begin, and allow your feelings to follow your obedience.

THE 5-PHASE JOURNEY

PHASE 1:
It Is Finished—But You're Not

SCRIPTURE & CORE TEACHING

Phase 1: It Is Finished—But You're Not

Scripture: *"When he had received the drink, Jesus said, 'It is finished.' With that, he bowed his head and gave up his spirit."* — John 19:30 (NIV)

The Truth You Need to Hear

Jesus completed His mission on the cross. He paid the price for your freedom in full: no payment plan required, no additional fees, no fine print. The work of salvation is finished, complete, and done. But here's what many people miss: just because His work is finished doesn't mean your journey is over.

Salvation is your starting point, not your finish line.

You are not working *for* your salvation; that battle has already been won and your spirit is secure in Christ. You are working *from* your salvation. There is still healing to walk through in your soul (mind, will, and emotions) and body, forgiveness to extend (both to others and yourself), purpose to discover, and freedom to fully embrace. Jesus handed you the baton when He said "It is finished." Now it's time to run your leg of the race.

This doesn't diminish what Christ accomplished. Instead, it honors it. When you choose to do the hard work of healing, when you refuse to stay stuck in patterns that don't serve you, when you courageously face your past to create a better future, you are living out the freedom He died to give you.

Understanding the Tension: Position vs. Process

Many Christians struggle with this tension:
If Jesus finished the work, why do I still hurt?
Why do I still struggle?
Why haven't my patterns changed automatically?

The answer lies in understanding the difference between **position** and **process**.

Your *position* before God is secure. Christ's work ensured that. You are already loved. Already chosen. Already redeemed. But the *process* of learning to live from that position — to embody it in your thoughts, patterns, and choices — takes time. It takes intention. It takes submission. It takes cooperation with the ongoing work of healing and transformation.

Think of it like this: when you receive the deed to a house, you legally own the property. But you still have to move in. You still have to learn where the light switches are, clean out what was left behind, and decide how to make it home. The ownership is settled. But the living in it — that's a process.

That was me.

I wanted to be free. I wanted healing. But I didn't want the process. I didn't want to go through the uncomfortable, messy, slow work of becoming well. I wanted the results without the journey. The freedom without the undoing.

But healing doesn't work like that.

There was so much hurt that had to be rooted out of me. So much shame. So much discontentment. And if I'm honest, there was self-hatred — a deep seeded belief that I was undeserving of good things. I had spent so long internalizing that belief that I began to live from it. Somewhere deep inside, I believed that I wasn't worthy of a better life. That lie became a root. And like any deeply tangled root, it couldn't be pulled up in a single tug. It had to be untangled gently, intentionally, over time.

And that takes process.

You don't just walk out of emotional captivity and instantly know how to live in freedom. Yes, Jesus sets you free. But **you still have to learn how to live free.**

Remember the Israelites? Their journey from Egypt to the Promised Land should have taken two weeks. Instead, it took forty years. And while we often criticize that delay, I've come to believe it might not have been wasted time. They had spent *hundreds* of years in slavery. Perhaps it took that long to unlearn the mindset of captivity. You don't leave bondage without some undoing. You don't shake off generational pain in a moment.

I used to feel ashamed when well-meaning people asked me, *"How long will you stay in the wilderness?"* I wanted to hurry up and be whole just to prove I could. But I wasn't submitting to the process — I was rushing toward results. And that's not the same thing.

The truth is, healing is slow. It is layered. It is not linear.
It is like trying to untangle a knotted string of Christmas lights —
you have to sit with it, take your time, work gently, and refuse to give up.

Your thoughts.
Your habits.
Your emotional reflexes.
Your old coping mechanisms.

All of those things are tangled.
And untangling takes time.

But it's okay. It's okay that it takes time.
It's okay that it's not instant.
It's okay that it's taking longer than you thought it would.
When I finally accepted that, I found peace.
And when I found peace, I could finally begin to heal for real.

The Baton Has Been Passed

When Jesus said *"It is finished,"* He completed His part of the divine relay race.
The baton of living out that freedom was passed to you.
This isn't about earning what He already provided; it's about stepping into what's already yours.

Your part of the race includes:

- Learning to think from your new identity instead of your old wounds
- Practicing new responses to old triggers
- Choosing healing over hiding, even when it's uncomfortable
- Setting boundaries that protect what Christ purchased
- Forgiving others and yourself from the overflow of His forgiveness
- Discovering and walking in the purpose He has for your life

Today we're establishing the foundation: Christ finished the work of salvation, but you have the privilege and responsibility of walking it out. This isn't about performance or perfectionism; it's about partnership with God in the process of transformation.

DEEP REFLECTION QUESTIONS

Processing Your Starting Point

Take time to work through these questions honestly. There's no rush. Allow yourself to feel whatever emerges as you reflect.

1. Salvation vs. Healing Confusion

Describe a time when you confused being "saved" with being "completely healed." What did that look like in your life? How did it affect your relationship with God when you continued to struggle?

2. The Performance Trap

Complete these sentences honestly:

"I feel like I'm working FOR my salvation when I…"

"I am working FROM my salvation when I..."

....

....

....

3. Your Relay Race Moment

If Jesus physically handed you a baton today with "It is finished" written on it, what would you do with it? Where would you run? What would your leg of the race look like?

....

....

....

....

....

....

4. Identifying Your Patterns

What patterns in your life suggest you're still trying to earn what Jesus already provided? (Examples: perfectionism, people-pleasing, workaholism, inability to rest, constant guilt)

....

....

....

....

....

5. The Freedom You're Not Living

What freedoms that Christ purchased for you are you not fully living in? Be specific.

....

....

....

....

....

6. Your Biggest Fear

What's your biggest fear about stepping into the fullness of what Christ accomplished for you?

....

....

....

....

....

PERSONAL APPLICATION EXERCISES

Moving from Earning to Living

Exercise 1: The Performance Audit

Check all that currently apply to your life:

- ☐ I feel like I have to prove my worth to God
- ☐ I work harder in spiritual disciplines when I feel distant from God
- ☐ I equate my performance with my standing before God
- ☐ I feel guilty when I struggle or fail
- ☐ I believe God loves me more when I'm "doing better"
- ☐ I'm afraid to rest because I might disappoint God
- ☐ I compare my spiritual life to others
- ☐ I feel like I need to "pay God back" for what He's done

For each item you checked, write one way you could shift from "earning" to "living out" your salvation:

1.
2.
3.
4.

Exercise 2: Your Identity Shift

Old Identity Statements
(Write thoughts that come from your wounds/past):

"I am…"

....

"I always…"

....

"I can't…"

....

"I'm not…"

....

New Identity Statements
(Write who you are because of Christ's finished work):

"Because of what Christ accomplished, I am…"

....

"Because I'm working FROM salvation, I can…"

....

"My new pattern is…"

....

"I am becoming…"

....

Exercise 3: The Deed to Your House

Using the house analogy from the teaching, complete these statements:

The deed I've been given (what Christ secured for me):

....

....

....

Rooms I'm already living in (areas where I experience freedom):

....

....

....

Rooms I haven't moved into yet (areas needing growth):

....

....

....

The first room I want to explore this week:

....

....

....

IDENTIFYING YOUR STARTING POINT

Where Are You Really Starting From?

Current Spiritual Health Inventory

Rate each area from 1-10, where: 1 = I'm working hard to earn this from God 10 = I'm living freely from what Christ provided

God's Love for Me: ___/10 How much do you live from the security of His unconditional love vs. trying to earn it?

My Worth and Value: ___/10 How much do you rest in your identity in Christ vs. working to prove your value?

Forgiveness (Self): ___/10 How much do you live from the forgiveness Christ provided vs. carrying guilt and shame?

Forgiveness (Others): ___/10 How much do you forgive from the overflow of His forgiveness vs. holding grudges?

Spiritual Freedom: ___/10 How much do you experience joy in your relationship with God vs. obligation and fear?

Emotional Health: ___/10 How much do you process emotions from security vs. being overwhelmed by them?

Life Purpose: ___/10 How much do you live from calling and passion vs. duty and performance?

Rest and Sabbath: ___/10 How much do you rest from accomplishment vs. feeling guilty when you're not productive?

Your Three Lowest Scores

(These are your priority areas for this journey):

1. _________________________ Score: __ Why do you think this area is challenging for you?

....

....

....

2. _________________________ Score: __ Why do you think this area is challenging for you?

....

....

....

3. _________________________ Score: __ Why do you think this area is challenging for you?

....

....

....

Your Foundation Areas

Your Three Highest Scores

(These are strengths you can build on):

1. _______________________ Score: __ How can this strength support growth in your lower-scoring areas?

....

2. _______________________ Score: __ How can this strength support growth in your lower-scoring areas?

....

3. _______________________ Score: __ How can this strength support growth in your lower-scoring areas?

....

The One Thing

If God could help you shift from "working for" to "working from" salvation in just one area during these 5 days, what would you want it to be?

....

....

....

....

....

ACTION PLANNING & PRAYER

Your Day 1 Commitments

This Week I Will Practice "Working From" Salvation By:

Choose 2-3 specific, measurable actions you'll take this week:

1. ____

How will you measure this? _____________________ When will you do this? _____________________

2. ____

How will you measure this? _____________________ When will you do this? _____________________

3. ____

How will you measure this? _____________________ When will you do this? _____________________

Shifting Your Internal Dialogue

Old Thought Pattern to Replace: "____"

New Truth to Practice: "_______________________________________"

When will you practice this new thought?

....

Accountability and Support

Who will you share these commitments with?

....

When will you check in with them?

....

What support do you need to be successful?

....

....

....

Prayer Focus for the Week

Personal Prayer Based on Today's Insights:

Dear Lord,

....

....

....

....

....

....

....

....

....

In Jesus' name, amen.

Daily Affirmation

Create a personal affirmation based on working FROM salvation rather than FOR it:

"Because of what Christ finished for me, I am _________________"

Where will you place this affirmation so you see it daily?

....

....

Celebration Plan

How will you celebrate taking this step of faith in beginning your healing journey?

....

....

....

....

....

ADDITIONAL REFLECTION SPACE

Additional Insights and Thoughts

Use this space for any additional reflections, insights, prayers, or thoughts that emerged during today's work. You might also use this space to process emotions that came up or to continue any of the exercises from earlier pages.

Phase 2 Preparation

Before beginning Phase 2, take a moment to:

- Review your commitments from today
- Notice any resistance or excitement about tomorrow's topic
- Pray for openness to what God wants to teach you
- Remember: you're stepping forward in faith, not waiting to feel ready

One thing I want to remember from today:

....

....

....

I will approach Phase 2 with:

....

....

....

....

....

....

....

End of Phase 1

"For it is by grace you have been saved, through faith—and this is not from yourselves, it is the gift of God—not by works, so that no one can boast. For we are God's handiwork, created in Christ Jesus to do good works, which God prepared in advance for us to do." — Ephesians 2:8-10 (NIV)

You have taken a significant step forward in faith today. Rest in what Christ has accomplished while embracing the journey of walking it out.

PHASE 2:
No One Else Is Coming

Phase 2: No One Else Is Coming

Scripture: *"When Jesus saw him lying there and learned that he had been in this condition for a long time, he asked him, 'Do you want to get well?'"* — John 5:6 (NIV)

The Question That Changes Everything

In John 5, Jesus encounters a man who had been lying by the Pool of Bethesda for thirty-eight years. Surrounded by others waiting for a miracle, he had grown used to watching people get ahead of him — and likely, used to being overlooked.

Instead of immediately healing him, Jesus asked a question that strikes deeper than the surface: *"Do you want to get well?"*
It seems like an obvious question. Of course he wanted to get well, right? He had been in that condition for decades. But Jesus wasn't questioning his *desire* as much as He was confronting his *readiness* — because healing doesn't just change your body. It changes your life. And that change requires participation.

Sometimes we wait for rescue when what we really need is a revelation: **Jesus already saved you.**
The emergency response team isn't coming because the emergency is over.
There's no Plan B because Plan A already worked perfectly.
It's your turn to pick up your mat and walk.

Jesus knew something we often forget: sometimes we get comfortable with our discomfort. Sometimes we grow attached to our struggles because they've become our identity. Sometimes we secretly prefer the familiar prison to the unfamiliar freedom.

The man had an excuse ready: *"I have no one to help me into the pool."* Sound familiar?
We all have our version of that excuse.
If only they would change.
If only I had more money.
If only my childhood had been different.

If only someone would finally understand me.

But Jesus' response cuts through all of it: *"Get up. Pick up your mat and walk."*
No one else was coming to fix the man's situation — and no one else is coming to fix yours either.
God has already made the way. Now you must choose to walk in it.

The Comfort of Familiar Dysfunction

After thirty-eight years, the man's spot by the pool had become home. He knew where to sleep. He knew how to get food. He knew who would help him. His disability had become both his identity and his safety net. Healing would cost him everything familiar. Even if what was familiar was painful.

That was true for me too.

There came a point in my own journey when I realized I had grown attached to the pain I knew. Letting go of familiar dysfunction felt harder than staying in it. I had spent so many years learning how to be hurt. How to survive. How to stay small. I knew how to be the victim. I knew how to get my feelings hurt. I knew what to expect in painful dynamics, and—strangely—there was comfort in that. The predictability of pain felt safer than the risk of something new.

I didn't know what healing would look like. I couldn't picture the other side. The strength people said I had? I couldn't see it yet. I wasn't sure I even believed it was there. So emotionally, staying in that place felt more secure than stepping into the unknown.

But breaking free changed everything.

It brought a level of freedom I didn't know was possible. It gave me clarity, peace, and strength I had never fully accessed. It's been the most beautiful and transformative journey. One I never imagined I'd walk, yet one I'm so thankful I did.

Many of us operate the same way.

We say we want change. We say we're tired of hurting. But we cling to what we've always known. We build our identity around our wounds, our excuses, and our limitations. We know how to be the overwhelmed one. The silenced one. The person who "can't help it." But we don't know—yet—how to be whole.

Healing means losing the familiar version of yourself. It means releasing the story you've told about why you can't move forward. It means taking responsibility for your life in ways that might feel terrifying.

But the other side of healing is worth it.
Freedom is worth it.
You are worth it.

The Excuse Inventory

The man at the pool blamed his circumstances: no one to help him, others getting ahead of him, the system being unfair. But Jesus didn't address any of those external factors. Instead, He focused on the man's willingness to be responsible for his own healing.

Your excuses might sound different:

- "I'm too damaged by my past"
- "My family doesn't support my growth"
- "I don't have the resources other people have"
- "No one understands what I've been through"
- "I've tried everything and nothing works"
- "Other people have it easier than I do"

These statements might contain elements of truth, but they become excuses when we use them to avoid taking the steps available to us right now.

Taking Ownership Without Self-Blame

There is a crucial difference between taking responsibility and taking blame.
Responsibility says, "Regardless of how I got here, I have choices about how I move forward."
Blame says, "This is all my fault, and I should have known better."

You are not responsible for everything that happened to you. But you are responsible for what you do with what happened to you. You did not choose your wounds. But you can choose your healing. You cannot control other people's actions. But you can control your responses.

I had to learn this the hard way.

For years, I was an expert at blaming myself. I blamed myself for everything that happened inside of my relationship. I blamed myself for what I tolerated. I blamed myself for what I did not know then but have learned since. I blamed myself for the ways I reacted under pressure. I blamed myself for staying. I blamed myself for leaving. I blamed myself for the silence I kept. I blamed myself for the words I said. I blamed myself for the words I didn't say. I blamed myself for things that were never my fault.

Even when I intellectually knew I was not responsible for all of it, I still carried blame in my body and in my mind. That blame created a cycle that kept me stuck for years. It convinced me that maybe I deserved what I experienced. That maybe something was wrong with me. That maybe my pain was the result of my worth (or lack thereof), or a failure in my character rather than the result of unhealed trauma and unhealthy dynamics.

Those lies held me hostage.

Even after I put physical distance between myself and the situation, there was still so much emotional distance I had not yet traveled. My body had left, but my mind and my heart were still trapped in a place I had outgrown. I was free on the outside but still bound on the inside. And I could not heal while carrying blame that never belonged to me.

Taking responsibility for my healing required releasing the blame I had carried for far too long. It required accepting that growth does not come from shame. It comes from truth. It comes from compassion. It comes from allowing God to rewrite the story I told myself about who I was and why things happened the way they did.

Letting go of blame did not excuse what happened. It freed me from the weight of believing I had caused it.

And in that freedom, healing finally had room to begin.

The Authority You Already Have

When Jesus told the man to get up and walk, He was revealing authority the man already possessed but hadn't recognized. The power to stand wasn't something Jesus gave him in that moment; it was something He helped him discover he'd had all along.

You have more power than you realize. You have the authority to:

- Choose your thoughts and responses
- Set boundaries that protect your peace
- Seek help and resources for your healing
- End relationships that harm you
- Forgive those who hurt you (for your freedom, not theirs)
- Change patterns that no longer serve you
- Pursue dreams that align with your calling

Today's Challenge

Today's challenge is to stop waiting for someone else to rescue you and start recognizing the rescue that's already happened. Christ has already provided everything you need for life and godliness (2 Peter 1:3). The question isn't whether help is available; it's whether you'll accept responsibility for accessing it.

DEEP REFLECTION QUESTIONS

Processing Your Rescue Expectations

Take time to work through these questions with complete honesty. Notice any resistance or defensiveness that arises.

1. Your Comfort Zone Inventory

What aspects of your current situation have become familiar, even if they're painful? Sometimes we can get so used to certain struggles that the idea of change feels scary, even when we want healing. What fears might you have about your life being different?

....

....

....

....

....

2. The Excuses You Use

Complete this sentence five different ways: "I can't move forward in my healing because..."

    1.

    2.

    3.

    4.

    5.

Now, for each excuse, write one small step you could take despite that limitation:

    1.

    2.

    3.

    4.

    5.

3. Who Are You Waiting For?

Who or what are you waiting to change before you can move forward? Be specific.

....

....

....

....

What would happen if that person or situation never changed? How would you live differently?

....

....

....

....

4. Your Identity Investment

How has your struggle become part of your identity? What would you lose if you were completely healed?

....

....

....

....

5. The Question Jesus Asks You

If Jesus asked you directly, "Do you want to get well?" what would your honest answer be? What fears or hesitations would you have?

6. Your Mat

What is your "mat" - the thing you need to pick up and carry as you move forward? What would walking away from your current situation look like practically?

PERSONAL APPLICATION EXERCISES

Taking Ownership of Your Healing

Exercise 1: Excuse vs. Reason Assessment

For each statement below, determine if it's currently functioning as an excuse (keeping you stuck) or a reason (explaining circumstances while still moving forward). Mark E for Excuse or R for Reason:

___ "My childhood trauma affects how I relate to people" ___ "I don't have time to focus on healing right now" ___ "My spouse doesn't support my growth" ___ "I've been hurt too many times to trust again" ___ "I don't have money for therapy or coaching" ___ "My family wouldn't understand if I changed" ___ "I'm too old to start over" ___ "I don't know where to begin"

For each item you marked as an excuse, write one way to reframe it as a reason while still taking action:

1.
2.
3.
4.

Exercise 2: Your Sphere of Influence

Draw three circles - one inside the other, like a target.

Inner Circle - Direct Control: List things you have complete control over (your thoughts, responses, choices, actions)
Middle Circle - Influence: List things you can influence but not control (relationships, work environment, family dynamics)
Outer Circle - No Control: List things outside your control (other people's choices, the past, natural circumstances)

Now identify: Where have you been focusing most of your energy? Where should you focus to move forward?

Exercise 3: The Authority Audit

Check the areas where you're currently exercising your God-given authority:

- ☐ Choosing my thoughts intentionally
- ☐ Setting healthy boundaries
- ☐ Seeking help when needed
- ☐ Ending harmful relationships
- ☐ Forgiving for my own freedom
- ☐ Changing destructive patterns
- ☐ Pursuing my calling and dreams
- ☐ Taking care of my physical health
- ☐ Managing my time and energy
- ☐ Speaking truth in love

Choose three unchecked areas to begin exercising authority this week:

1.

First step: _______________________________________

2.

First step: _______________________________________

3.

First step: _______________________________________

TAKING OWNERSHIP ASSESSMENT

Where Do You Need to Stop Waiting?

Relationship Ownership

Rate from 1-10 (1 = completely waiting for others to change, 10 = taking full ownership):

With my spouse/partner: ___/10 What am I waiting for them to change? _______________________
What can I control in this relationship? _______________________________________

With my children: ___/10 What am I waiting for them to change? _____________________________
What can I control in this relationship? _______________________________________

With my parents/family: ___/10 What am I waiting for them to change? _______________________
What can I control in this relationship? _______________________________________

With friends: ___/10 What am I waiting for them to change? _________________________________
What can I control in this relationship? _______________________________________

At work: ___/10 What am I waiting for them to change? _____________________________________
What can I control in this situation? ____

Life Area Ownership

Physical Health: ___/10 What am I waiting for? ____
What action can I take? _______________________________________

Financial Health: ___/10 What am I waiting for? ____
What action can I take? _______________________________________

Emotional Health: ___/10 What am I waiting for? ____
What action can I take? _______________________________________

Spiritual Growth: ___/10 What am I waiting for? ____
What action can I take? _______________________________________

Career/Purpose: ___/10 What am I waiting for? ____
What action can I take? _______________________________________

Your Lowest Ownership Scores

The three areas where you're most stuck waiting:

1. _______________________ Score: ___
What's one step you could take this week regardless of others' actions?

....

2. _______________________ Score: ___
What's one step you could take this week regardless of others' actions?

....

3. _______________________ Score: ___
What's one step you could take this week regardless of others' actions?

....

The One Decision

If you could make one decision today that would demonstrate you're no longer waiting for rescue, what would it be?

....

....

....

....

....

....

ACTION PLANNING & PRAYER

Your Phase 2 Commitments

This Week I Will Stop Waiting and Start Acting By:

Choose 2-3 specific actions that demonstrate ownership:

1. ____ Timeline: _________________________________ How I'll measure success: _____________________

2. ____ Timeline: _________________________________ How I'll measure success: _____________________

3. ____ Timeline: _________________________________ How I'll measure success: _____________________

Breaking the Excuse Pattern

My most frequent excuse: "____"

The truth behind this excuse:

....

....

....

....

My new response when this excuse arises: "____"

Responsibility Without Shame

Something I need to take responsibility for:

....

How I'll do this without self-blame:

....

....

The grace I need to extend to myself:

....

....

Support and Accountability

Who I'll tell about my ownership commitments:

....

....

When we'll check in:

....

....

What support I need to be successful:

....

....

Prayer for Ownership

Heavenly Father,

Help me see the difference between what I can and cannot control. Give me the courage to take responsibility for my part while releasing what belongs to You or others.

When I'm tempted to make excuses, remind me of the authority You've given me. When I want to wait for someone else to change, redirect my focus to what I can do.

Give me wisdom to know the difference between responsibility and blame. Help me move forward without condemning myself for where I've been.

I choose to pick up my mat and walk. Meet me in my movement.

In Jesus' name, amen.

Personal Prayer Space

Write your own prayer about taking ownership of your healing:

....

....

....

....

....

....

Daily Declaration

"I will no longer wait for ___________________ to change. Instead, I will ___________________ __________."

When will you speak this declaration daily?

....

....

ADDITIONAL REFLECTION SPACE

Additional Insights and Processing

Use this space for continued reflection, emotional processing, or expanding on any of today's exercises. You might also want to explore any resistance you felt to taking ownership.

Celebrating Ownership

One way I took ownership today:

....

How it felt to stop making excuses:

....

....

What I learned about my own authority:

....

....

Phase 3 Preparation

Before beginning Phase 3, reflect on:

- How did taking ownership feel today?
- What resistance came up?
- Where do you sense God leading you next?

One insight I want to carry into tomorrow:

....

....

I will approach Phase 3 with this attitude:

....

....

....

End of Phase 2

"Therefore, my dear friends, as you have always obeyed—not only in my presence, but now much more in my absence—continue to work out your salvation with fear and trembling, for it is God who works in you to will and to act in order to fulfill his good purpose." — Philippians 2:12-13 (NIV)

You have chosen to stop waiting and start walking. That's a profound act of faith and courage. Rest in the truth that as you take responsibility for your part, God is working in you for His good purpose.

PHASE 3:
You Don't Have to Do the Healing

Phase 3: You Don't Have to Do the Healing

Scripture: *"He heals the brokenhearted and binds up their wounds."* — Psalm 147:3 (NIV)

The Relief You've Been Looking For

Here's something that might surprise you: God never asked you to heal yourself. That's His job. He's the Healer; you're the patient. Your role is not to perform surgery on your own heart but to be present in the process: open, honest, surrendered, and willing.

You may not have the strength to fix what's broken inside you, but you do have the strength to surrender it to the One who specializes in impossible restoration. You don't have to figure out how to untangle decades of pain. You don't have to have the perfect words for your prayers. You don't have to understand the timeline or the process.

Healing doesn't mean you're in control; it means you're cooperating with the One who is.

Think of it like this: when you go to a doctor for a broken bone, you don't heal the bone yourself. You show up to the appointments, follow the treatment plan, rest when instructed, and do the physical therapy. But the actual knitting together of bone happens through processes beyond your control. Your body knows how to heal; it just needs the right conditions. The same is true for emotional and spiritual healing. God built you with an incredible capacity for restoration, but healing happens best when you create the right environment:

- honesty about your pain
- willingness to feel difficult emotions
- openness to His process
- patience with His timing.

The Difference Between Doing and Cooperating

Yesterday we talked about taking ownership — about not waiting around for someone to come rescue you. Today, we hold that in tension with the necessity of surrender. This isn't contradictory; it's complementary.

You take ownership of creating the conditions for healing while surrendering the actual healing work to God.

Your Part:

- Show up consistently
- Be honest about your pain
- Follow wise counsel
- Create healthy boundaries
- Engage in practices that support healing

God's Part:

- The actual healing
- Transformation of your heart
- Restoration of your capacity to love and trust
- Renewal of your mind
- Redemption of your story

But here's where many people — myself included — get stuck.
Some of us exhaust ourselves trying to do God's part, striving for results only He can bring.
Others, like me for much of my journey, **wait passively** for God to do everything, while quietly neglecting our responsibility to **cooperate** with the process.

I was the latter.
I hoped.
I wished.
I wanted things to change... desperately.
But I wasn't actually *doing* anything to create the environment for change.

I said all the right things, but I wasn't setting up healthy boundaries.
I listened to wise words, but my heart wasn't receiving them.
I prayed, but I also lied to myself, telling myself I could handle things I knew were too much emotionally.
I was sowing mixed seed: speaking life in one breath and stepping back into dysfunction the next.
And when things didn't change, I blamed the process or blamed God... when deep down, I hadn't fully shown up for my part.

Let me be clear — this isn't self-blame. This is accountability wrapped in compassion.

I *thought* I was actively participating in my healing, but what I was really doing was hoping for change without changing anything. I didn't want to set limits. I didn't want to walk away. I didn't want to feel lonely. I wanted to feel different **without doing the work that feeling different required.**

And the truth is, **it doesn't work that way.**
Healing isn't magic. It's sacred collaboration.
God is willing — but you must be willing too.

When You're Trying Too Hard

Many of us unknowingly try to do God's job in the healing process. The signs can be subtle but telling.

You might feel exhausted by your healing efforts or frustrated that change isn't happening fast enough. You may find yourself analyzing every emotion and trying to fix yourself constantly. You feel guilty when you're not actively working on healing — as if rest is a betrayal of progress. You believe healing depends entirely on your effort and understanding. You grow impatient with God's timing and process.

This kind of self-focused healing effort often comes from good intentions, but it can actually hinder the process. When we're consumed with managing our healing, we're not surrendered to the Healer.

The Art of Surrender

Surrender isn't passivity; it's active trust. It's choosing to believe that God's process is better than your plan, His timing is wiser than your urgency, and His methods are more effective than your efforts.

Surrender means:

- Releasing the need to understand everything before you obey
- Trusting God's timeline even when it feels too slow
- Being honest about your pain without trying to immediately fix it
- Following His guidance even when it doesn't make sense to you
- Accepting that healing happens in layers, not all at once
- Allowing yourself to feel emotions without rushing to resolve them

Creating Conditions for Healing

While God does the healing, you create the conditions where healing can flourish:

Honesty: Being truthful about your real struggles, not the sanitized version
Presence: Staying present with difficult emotions instead of numbing or avoiding
Community: Surrounding yourself with people who support your growth
Rest: Allowing yourself to receive rather than constantly striving
Boundaries: Protecting the healing environment from toxic influences
Patience: Trusting the process even when progress feels slow
Faith: Believing God is working even when you can't see evidence

God's Heart for Your Healing

God is not reluctant to heal you. He's not withholding healing until you perform better or understand more. His heart toward you is compassionate, patient, and committed to your wholeness. He's more invested in your healing than you are.

God will also not rush the process. He is a gentleman and will move at the pace that you are willing to move at. He is patient and will walk alongside you in the present as you sift through your past and move toward your future. When you get off course, He stays on the path and awaits your return to begin the healing journey again. He takes His place right beside you, gently encouraging you, lovingly nudging you, and wholeheartedly believing in your ability to walk out your healing.

Sometimes we unconsciously believe we have to convince God to heal us or earn His willingness to restore us. But Psalm 147:3 doesn't say He heals the worthy or the deserving; it says He heals the brokenhearted. Your brokenness is your qualification, not your disqualification.

Today's Focus

Today we're learning to rest in God's role as Healer while faithfully fulfilling our role as willing participants. We're releasing the burden of fixing ourselves while embracing the responsibility of cooperating with His work in our lives.

DEEP REFLECTION QUESTIONS

Processing Your Relationship with Healing

Take time to honestly explore your beliefs and patterns around healing work.

1. Your Healing Beliefs

What do you believe about who is responsible for your healing? Where did these beliefs come from?

2. The Burden You've Been Carrying

In what ways have you been trying to do God's job in your healing? How has this affected your relationship with Him and with yourself?

3. Control vs. Surrender

Complete these sentences:

"I try to control my healing by…"

....

....

"I would surrender my healing to God if…"

....

....

"My biggest fear about letting God control my healing process is…"

....

....

....

4. Exhaustion Assessment

Are you exhausted by your healing efforts? If so, what specifically is draining you?

....

....

....

....

5. God's Heart Toward You

How do you honestly believe God feels about your brokenness? About your healing journey? Write what you think versus what Scripture says.

What I think: ______________________________

....

What Scripture says: ____________________________

....

6. Your Cooperation Style

How do you naturally approach cooperation with God? Are you more likely to be passive (waiting for Him to do everything) or controlling (trying to manage the process)?

....

....

....

....

7. The Conditions You're Creating

Looking at the list of healing conditions (honesty, presence, community, rest, boundaries, patience, faith), which ones are you actively creating? Which ones are you avoiding?

Creating well: ______________________________

....

Need to develop: ____________________________

....

PERSONAL APPLICATION EXERCISES

Learning to Cooperate with the Healer

Exercise 1: Role Clarity Assessment

For each healing activity below, mark whether it's primarily Your Job (Y), God's Job (G), or Shared (S):

__ Showing up to therapy appointments __ Transforming your heart __ Setting healthy boundaries __ Healing childhood trauma __ Being honest about your struggles __ Changing your automatic reactions __ Reading books about healing __ Removing shame and guilt __ Practicing forgiveness __ Restoring your ability to trust __ Creating supportive relationships __ Renewing your mind __ Choosing vulnerability over hiding __ Healing your emotional wounds

Review your answers. Where have you been trying to do God's job? Where have you been avoiding your job?

....

....

....

Exercise 2: Surrender Practice

Something I need to surrender to God's control:

....

My fear about surrendering this:

....

....

....

How I'll practice surrender this week:

....

....

....

....

Prayer of Surrender: *God, I surrender _____________________ to Your healing process.*

I trust that You __________ ______________________________. Help me to _____________________.

Exercise 3: Creating Healing Conditions

Rate yourself 1-10 in each area:

Honesty (being real about your struggles): __/10 One way to improve: _____________________

Presence (staying with difficult emotions): __/10 One way to improve: _____________________

Community (surrounding yourself with support): __/10 One way to improve: _____________________

Rest (allowing yourself to receive): __/10 One way to improve: _____________________

Boundaries (protecting your healing space): __/10 One way to improve: _____________________

Patience (trusting God's timing): __/10 One way to improve: _____________________

Faith (believing God is working): __/10 One way to improve: _____________________

Choose your lowest score and create a specific plan to improve it this week:

Area: _____________________ Specific action: _____________________

When: _____________________ How you'll measure progress: _____________________

SURRENDER PRACTICE WORKSHEETS

Learning to Let God Heal

Surrender Assessment

Areas where I'm trying too hard to heal myself:

1.

How this shows up: _________________________ What surrender would look like: _______________

2.

How this shows up: _________________________ What surrender would look like: _______________

3.

How this shows up: _________________________ What surrender would look like: _______________

Trust Building Exercise

Past evidence of God's faithfulness in my life:

1.
2.
3.

How this evidence can help me trust His healing process:

....

....

....

....

Patience Practice

An area where I'm impatient with God's timing:

....

What this impatience costs me:

....

....

A prayer for patience: *God, help me trust Your timing with* ________________________.

When I'm tempted to rush ahead, remind me that ________________________.

Cooperation Plan

This week I will cooperate with God's healing by:

Showing up: ________________ (appointments, practices, commitments)

Being honest: ________________ (about struggles, needs, emotions)

Creating space: ________________ (for rest, reflection, processing)

Following guidance: ________________ (from Scripture, wise counsel, Holy Spirit)

Practicing presence: ________________ (staying with emotions instead of avoiding)

Daily Surrender Practice

Choose a daily practice to remind yourself that God is the Healer:

- ☐ Morning prayer surrendering the day's healing to God
- ☐ Evening reflection on how you cooperated with His work
- ☐ Reading Psalm 147:3 and personalizing it
- ☐ Setting a phone reminder to surrender control
- ☐ Journaling about what you're releasing to God
- ☐ Other: ________________________

When will you practice this daily habit?

....

What will help you remember?

....

Releasing the Burden

Complete this statement:

"I am releasing the burden of ____

to God because He is _______________________________ *and I trust Him to* _______________________________*."*

Write this surrender statement where you'll see it daily:

....

....

....

....

....

....

....

ACTION PLANNING & PRAYER

Your Day 3 Commitments

This Week I Will Cooperate with God's Healing By:

Choose 2-3 specific ways you'll create conditions for healing while surrendering the results:

1. ____ How this cooperates with God: ________________

Timeline: _______________________________

2. ____ How this cooperates with God: ________________

Timeline: _______________________________

3. ____ How this cooperates with God: ________________

Timeline: _______________________________

Shifting from Control to Cooperation

Something I need to stop trying to control:

....

How I'll practice surrender with this:

....

....

Something I need to take more responsibility for:

....

....

How I'll step up in this area:

....

....

Creating Healing Conditions

The healing condition I most need to develop:

....

My specific plan for this week:

....

....

How I'll know I'm making progress:

....

Support and Accountability

Who I'll share my surrender commitments with:

....

How they can support me:

....

When we'll check in:

....

Prayer for Surrender and Cooperation

Heavenly Father,

I acknowledge that You are the Healer and I am the patient. Forgive me for trying to do Your job and neglecting my own.

Help me surrender _______________________ to Your healing process. I release my need to control the timeline, understand the methods, or manage the results.

Show me how to faithfully cooperate with Your work by creating the right conditions for healing. Give me wisdom to know when to act and when to rest, when to push forward and when to be patient.

I trust that You are more invested in my healing than I am. Help me believe that Your heart toward me is good, Your timing is perfect, and Your methods are wise.

Heal what I cannot heal. Restore what I cannot restore. Transform what I cannot change.

In Jesus' name, amen.

Personal Prayer Space

Write your own prayer about surrendering to God's healing process:

....

....

....

....

....

....

Daily Affirmation

"God is my Healer. My job is to ____.

His job is to ________________________________."

When will you speak this affirmation daily?

....

....

....

Celebration and Rest

How will you celebrate choosing surrender over control?

....

....

....

How will you practice rest this week as an act of faith?

....

....

....

....

ADDITIONAL REFLECTION SPACE

Additional Insights and Processing

Use this space for continued reflection on surrender, any emotions that arose, or insights about God's role as Healer versus your role as participant.

Noticing God's Work

Evidence I've seen this week that God is working in my healing:

....

....

....

....

How surrendering control felt different from trying to manage everything:

....

....

....

....

One way I experienced God's heart toward my brokenness:

....

....

....

....

Before beginning phase 4, reflect on:

- How did practicing surrender affect your stress level?
- What did you learn about cooperation versus control?
- Where do you sense God leading you to take action next?

One thing I want to remember about God as my Healer:

....

....

....

I will approach Day 4 with this understanding:

....

....

....

End of Phase 3

"Come to me, all you who are weary and burdened, and I will give you rest. Take my yoke upon you and learn from me, for I am gentle and lowly in heart, and you will find rest for your souls. For my yoke is easy and my burden is light." — Matthew 11:28-30 (NIV)

You have chosen to release the burden of healing yourself and trust the gentle heart of your Healer. Rest in His competence and faithfulness as you cooperate with His good work in your life.

PHASE 4:
Healing Requires Movement

SCRIPTURE & CORE TEACHING

Phase 4: Healing Requires Movement

Scripture: *"In the same way, faith by itself, if it is not accompanied by action, is dead."* — James 2:17 (NIV)

The Partnership Between Faith and Action

Healing is not a passive experience. While you don't have to do the healing (that's God's part), you do have to participate in it. Faith without works is dead, and healing without movement is stagnant.

It's one intentional step at a time: through prayer that's honest about your struggles, through counseling that addresses root issues, through journaling that processes your emotions, through choosing healthier responses to old triggers. Movement matters because while God is faithful to meet you wherever you are, He also invites you to press forward toward the calling He has placed on your life.

You can pray for healing and still need to go to therapy. You can believe in God's power and still take medication for depression. You can trust in divine restoration and still need to set boundaries with toxic people. You can have faith in God's plan and still need to forgive those who hurt you. These aren't contradictions; they're collaborations.

God's Ordinary Means

God often works through ordinary means to accomplish extraordinary healing. The therapist who helps you process trauma, the friend who holds you accountable, the book that gives you new perspective, the decision to finally say no to what's harming you; these can all be instruments of His healing in your life.

Don't despise the practical steps because they seem too simple or too human. God uses ordinary obedience to create miraculous transformation. He doesn't always work through dramatic supernatural interventions. Often, His healing comes through the consistent choice to do the next right thing.

The same God who parted the Red Sea also told the Israelites to walk through it. The same God who provided manna also required them to gather it daily. The same God who heals your heart also calls you to engage in practices that support that healing.

Movement vs. Striving

There's an important distinction between movement and striving. Movement is responsive action; striving is anxious effort. Movement flows from faith; striving flows from fear. Movement trusts God's process; striving tries to control outcomes.

Healing Movement Looks Like:

- Taking steps based on wisdom and guidance
- Acting from rest rather than anxiety
- Engaging in healthy practices consistently
- Making choices aligned with your healing values
- Following through on commitments to yourself
- Seeking help when you need it
- Creating environments that support growth

Healing Striving Looks Like:

- Desperately trying multiple approaches at once
- Constantly analyzing your progress
- Feeling panicked when change feels slow
- Exhausting yourself with healing activities
- Comparing your timeline to others
- Feeling guilty when you rest or have fun
- Making your healing an idol

The Rhythm of Healing Action

Healthy healing has rhythm: seasons of active work and seasons of rest, times of breakthrough and times of integration, periods of learning new skills and periods of practicing familiar ones.

You don't have to be constantly working on healing to be making progress. Sometimes the most healing thing you can do is rest, play, enjoy relationships, or engage in activities that have nothing to do with your issues. Healing happens in the margins as much as in the focused work.

Types of Healing Movement

Physical Movement: Exercise, proper nutrition, adequate sleep, medical care, body work
Emotional Movement: Therapy, support groups, journaling, creative expression, feeling your feelings
Relational Movement: Setting boundaries, having honest conversations, building healthy relationships, ending toxic ones
Spiritual Movement: Prayer, worship, Scripture reading, spiritual direction, serving others
Mental Movement: Reading, learning new perspectives, challenging old thought patterns, developing new skills
Practical Movement: Organizing your environment, changing routines, making decisions you've avoided

When Movement Feels Impossible

Sometimes depression, trauma, or overwhelming circumstances make movement feel impossible. In these seasons, remember that even tiny steps count. Getting out of bed is movement. Taking a shower is movement. Calling a friend is movement. Asking for help is movement.

Don't despise small beginnings. God honors faithful action regardless of size. Often, the smallest steps in the darkest seasons require the most courage and produce the most significant healing over time.

I had plenty of those days—days where movement felt impossible. The seemingly smallest tasks required the maximum amount of effort. But I believe it's in those very seasons that God saw deeply into my effort. When I would have rather just curled up and given up, He saw me. He saw me trying. He saw me working. He saw me moving. And those small movements mattered just as much to Him as the days when I felt like I was clicking on all cylinders.

It all mattered. Every moment, every breath, every brave choice to not give up—it mattered.

And though I didn't know it at the time, it made the biggest difference in my heart. When I began to acknowledge the small steps I was taking, when I learned to have grace for myself, when I learned to persevere, when I started to applaud the slow, intentional progress—everything shifted.

It was like finally being able to look back and see that the journey of a thousand miles had, in fact, begun with one small step. And I hadn't let myself get stuck in the darkest part of the journey. I kept moving, one faithful step at a time, toward a light I couldn't see yet... but trusted was there.

Today's Focus

Today we're learning to recognize healing as an active process that requires your participation while trusting God's power to work through your obedience. We're identifying specific areas where you need to move forward and creating practical plans for taking action.

DEEP REFLECTION QUESTIONS

Processing Your Relationship with Action

Take time to honestly examine your patterns of movement and stillness in your healing journey.

1. Your Movement Pattern

Are you more likely to avoid action (waiting for healing to happen to you) or to over-function (trying to force healing through constant activity)? How has this pattern affected your progress?

2. Where You've Been Stuck

What areas of your healing have you been avoiding taking action on? What has kept you stuck?

3. Faith and Action Integration

Complete these sentences:

"I believe God wants to heal me, but I avoid taking action when…"

....

....

....

"I take action in my healing, but I struggle to trust God when…"

....

....

....

4. Ordinary Means Resistance

What practical healing resources (therapy, medication, support groups, boundaries, etc.) have you resisted because they don't feel "spiritual" enough? Why?

....

....

....

....

....

5. Movement vs. Striving Assessment

Describe a time when you were moving in healthy ways toward healing versus a time when you were striving. What was different about your motivation and approach?

Healthy Movement: _____________________

....

....

Unhealthy Striving: _____________________

....

....

6. Small Steps Recognition

What small steps have you taken in your healing that you haven't given yourself credit for?

....

....

....

....

7. Next Right Thing

If you could only take one healing action this week, what would be the most important "next right thing" for you?

....

....

....

PERSONAL APPLICATION EXERCISES

Creating Your Movement Plan

Exercise 1: Healing Action Audit

Rate yourself 1-10 in how actively you're engaged in each area:

Physical Health (exercise, nutrition, sleep, medical care): __/10

Current actions: _______________________ One improvement: _______________________

Emotional Health (therapy, journaling, processing feelings): __/10

Current actions: _______________________ One improvement: _______________________

Relational Health (boundaries, communication, healthy connections): __/10

Current actions: _______________________ One improvement: _______________________

Spiritual Health (prayer, Scripture, worship, service): __/10

Current actions: _______________________ One improvement: _______________________

Mental Health (learning, challenging thoughts, new perspectives): __/10

Current actions: _______________________ One improvement: _______________________

Practical Health (environment, routines, decision-making): __/10

Current actions: _______________________ One improvement: _______________________

Exercise 2: Movement vs. Avoidance

Actions I need to take but have been avoiding:

1.

Why I've avoided this: _______________________ One small step I could take: _______________________

2.

Why I've avoided this: _______________________ One small step I could take: _______________________

3.

Why I've avoided this: _______________________ One small step I could take: _______________________

Exercise 3: God's Ordinary Means

List people, resources, or opportunities God has placed in your life that could support your healing:

1.
2.
3.
4.
5.

Which of these have you been underutilizing? Why?

....

....

How will you better engage with these resources?

....

....

....

MOVEMENT PLANNING WORKSHEETS

Creating Your Action Steps

Priority Movement Areas

Based on your reflection, identify your top 3 areas needing movement:

Priority 1: _________________________________ **Why this matters:** _________________________________

Specific action: _________________________________ **Timeline:** _________________________________

How you'll measure progress: _________________________________

Priority 2: _________________________________ **Why this matters:** _________________________________

Specific action: _________________________________ **Timeline:** _________________________________

How you'll measure progress: _________________________________

Priority 3: _________________________________ **Why this matters:** _________________________________

Specific action: _________________________________ **Timeline:** _________________________________

How you'll measure progress: _________________________________

Breaking Down Overwhelming Actions

An action that feels too big to take:

....

Example: "I need to find a therapist and start counseling"

Break it into smaller steps:

Step 1: Ask friends for therapist recommendations
Step 2: Research therapists online and read reviews
Step 3: Check which therapists take my insurance
Step 4: Call 2-3 offices to ask about availability
Step 5: Schedule initial consultation with one therapist

Which step will you take first? Step 1 - Ask friends for recommendations **When?** This week

....

Now try it with your overwhelming action:

Break it into smaller steps:

      Step 1: _________________________________

      Step 2: _________________________________

      Step 3: _________________________________

      Step 4: _________________________________

      Step 5: _________________________________

Which step will you take first? _______________ **When?** _________________________________

Movement Rhythms

Active Seasons: Times when you engage intensively with healing work **Rest Seasons:** Times when you integrate, play, and live normally **Current Season:** What season are you in now? _________

If you're in an active season: What active work will you commit to? _______________ How will you avoid striving? _________________ When will you schedule rest? _________________

If you're in a rest season: How will you honor this season? _________________ What gentle maintenance will you continue? _____________ How will you know when to become more active? _________

Accountability and Support

Movement Partner: Who will support your action steps?

....

Check-in Schedule: When and how will you connect?

....

What support you need: What do you need from others to be successful?

....

....

Obstacle Planning

Likely obstacles to taking action:

1.

How you'll handle this: __________________

2.

How you'll handle this: __________________

3.

How you'll handle this: __________________

Your plan when motivation is low:

....

....

Your plan when progress feels slow:

....

....

....

ACTION PLANNING & PRAYER

Your Day 4 Commitments

This Week I Will Take Healing Action By:

Choose 2-3 specific, measurable actions:

1. ____ Deadline: _____________________________

Success looks like: _________________________________

2. ____ Deadline: _____________________________

Success looks like: _________________________________

3. ____ Deadline: _____________________________

Success looks like: _________________________________

From Avoidance to Action

Something I've been avoiding:

....

The first step I'll take this week:

....

What I'll do when resistance comes up:

....

How I'll celebrate taking this step:

....

Faith-Action Integration

How my actions this week will demonstrate faith in God's healing power:

....

....

Prayer I'll say before taking difficult actions:

....

....

Daily Movement Practice

One small daily action I'll commit to:

....

When I'll do this: _______________________________

How I'll remember: _______________________________

Movement Affirmation

Complete this statement: "God meets me in my movement. When I take the step of _______________,

I trust that He will _______________."

Support and Accountability

Who I'll tell about my action commitments:

....

How they can support me:

....

When we'll check in:

....

Prayer for Faith-Filled Action

Heavenly Father,

Thank You for healing that comes through both Your supernatural power and ordinary means. Help me embrace movement as cooperation with Your work in my life.

Give me courage to take the steps I've been avoiding. When I'm tempted to wait for perfect conditions or dramatic breakthroughs, remind me that You meet me in daily small consistent steps—moment by moment, one step at a time.

Help me distinguish between healthy movement and anxious striving. Show me when to act and when to rest, when to push forward and when to be patient.

Use my obedience, even in small things, to bring about the healing You have planned. Bless the ordinary steps I take with extraordinary results.

I trust that as I move in faith, You will work in power.

In Jesus' name, amen.

Personal Prayer Space

Write your own prayer about taking faith-filled action in your healing:

....

....

....

....

....

....

....

Movement Declaration

**"This week I choose movement over stagnation. I will trust God by taking the action of
_______________________ and believing He will meet me in that step."**

When will you speak this declaration daily?

....

....

....

....

....

ADDITIONAL REFLECTION SPACE

Additional Insights and Processing

Use this space for continued reflection on movement, action, and the integration of faith with practical steps. You might also explore any fears or resistance that came up around taking action.

Celebrating Action

One action I took today that moved me forward:

....

How it felt to choose movement over avoidance:

....

....

Evidence that God was with me in my action:

....

....

Learning from Movement

What I learned about myself through taking action:

....

....

How my relationship with God grew through movement:

....

....

One insight I want to remember about faith and action:

....

....

Tomorrow's Preparation

Before beginning Day 5, reflect on:

- How did taking action affect your hope and energy?
- What did you learn about God's presence in ordinary obedience?
- What momentum do you want to carry into the final day?

One commitment I want to maintain beyond this week:

....

....

I will approach Day 5 with this perspective:

....

....

End of Phase 4

"In their hearts humans plan their course, but the Lord establishes their steps." — Proverbs 16:9 (NIV)

You have chosen faithful action over passive waiting. God is establishing your steps and working through your obedience. Trust that every faithful step is building toward the wholeness He has planned for you.

PHASE 5:
Your Wholeness Is Worth the Work

Scripture and Core Teaching

Phase 5: Your Wholeness Is Worth the Work

Scripture: *"Beloved, I pray that you may prosper in all things and be in health, just as your soul prospers."* — 3 John 1:2 (NKJV)

Note: When John prays for prosperity "just as your soul prospers," he's praying for wholeness in your mind, will, and emotions to align with your spiritual health.

The Sacred Nature of Your Healing Journey

You Are Worth the Work

God doesn't want just part of you healed. He wants you whole—mind, body, and spirit. While the work may be hard, it is also holy. Your healing journey is sacred because it doesn't just transform you. It creates space for others to believe that their own healing is possible too.

Every journal entry where you process your truth...
Every prayer where you pour out your heart...
Every therapy session where you face what once felt unbearable...
Every boundary you set to protect your peace...

It all matters.

These moments aren't small. They are sacred. They are seeds—evidence of your faith taking root. The energy you're expending is not wasted; it is worship. The choices you're making are not insignificant; they are declarations that *you are worth the work.*

Wholeness is not a luxury reserved for those who had it easier. It is your inheritance as a child of God. And it is worth fighting for with everything you've got.

Because what you're doing? It's not ordinary.

You are disrupting generational cycles.
You are breaking soul ties and rewriting mental scripts.
You are confronting lies and birthing new truth.
You are changing the atmosphere of your lineage.

This is no small thing. It is *monumental*.

You are not just healing for you.
You are healing for the little girl inside you who thought she wasn't enough.
You are healing for the future you who refuses to shrink ever again.
You are healing for your children, your children's children...
And every future generation who carries your DNA.

And every step of that journey is proof that heaven believes you're worth it.

The Ripple Effect of Your Healing

Your healing is not just personal.
It's generational.
It's communal.
It's Kingdom-impacting.

Your children will inherit emotional health instead of generational trauma.
Your friends will witness what's possible when someone refuses to stay stuck.
Your community will benefit from the gifts that were buried under your pain—gifts now being uncovered through your courage.

The world needs what you carry.
But it can only receive it when you are whole enough to offer it from a place of overflow... not deficit.

The time you're investing in becoming whole is not selfish.
It's one of the most generous, legacy-building, cycle-breaking acts of love you could ever give.

When you break patterns of dysfunction, you're not just healing yourself.
You're healing your family line.
You're healing the ones connected to your life and legacy.

When you set healthy boundaries, you're modeling freedom for others who are silently drowning in guilt and people-pleasing.

When you choose forgiveness over bitterness, you create sacred space for others to believe forgiveness is possible.

Every single brave step you take becomes a blueprint someone else can follow.

There *will* be lives changed because of your testimony.
There *will* be yokes broken because of your obedience.
There *will* be generational patterns rewritten because of your surrender.

Your story will offer hope.
It will offer encouragement.
It will offer a glimpse into what is truly possible—*with God, healing is possible.*

So yes... your healing is for you.
But it's also for the ones watching.
For your neighbor who doesn't know how to ask for help.
For your sister who's silently struggling.
For the woman down the street who sees you and wonders if healing could be real for her too.
For the man in the store who's carrying invisible grief and doesn't have words for it yet.

Someone else's breakthrough is tied to your willingness to walk this out.
Their freedom is tethered to your faith.

This is weighty. This is holy. This is a call to rise.
Let this truth ignite urgency in your spirit.
Let it remind you that this work matters.
That *you* matter.

And that healing is not only available...
It's *worth everything it costs.*

What Wholeness Actually Means

Wholeness doesn't mean perfection. It doesn't mean you'll never struggle, never have difficult emotions, or never face challenges. Wholeness means your spirit, soul (mind, will, and emotions), and body are all functioning as God intended and working together in harmony.

This looks like:

Spirit: Secure relationship with God, living from your identity in Christ
Mind: Thoughts aligned with truth rather than lies, healthy thinking patterns
Will: Making choices based on values rather than fears or compulsions
Emotions: Feeling (your feelings) fully while not being controlled by emotions
Body: Physical health and caring for your body as God's temple

Wholeness is about becoming fully yourself: the person God created you to be before pain taught you to hide, perform, or settle for less.

The Cost and Value of Wholeness

The work of wholeness costs something. It costs comfort with familiar dysfunction. It costs the identity you've built around your wounds. It costs relationships that depend on you staying small. It costs the illusion that someone else will rescue you.

But what you gain is infinitely more valuable.

You gain:

- Freedom to live according to your values rather than your fears
- Capacity to love others without losing yourself
- Ability to pursue your calling without self-sabotage
- Energy that was previously consumed by managing pain
- Relationships based on mutual health rather than mutual dysfunction
- Legacy of healing for those who come after you

Why You're Worth the Investment

You might struggle to believe you're worth the effort that wholeness requires. You might think others deserve healing more than you do, that your wounds aren't significant enough to warrant attention, or that you should be grateful for any improvement rather than pursuing complete wholeness.

But God's desire for your prosperity in all things—including wholeness in your spirit, soul, and body—isn't conditional on your feelings of worthiness. It's based on His love and His vision for your life.

He had a vision, purpose, and plan for your life before the foundation of the earth was laid. He knows who He called you to be in spite of the struggles He knew you would face, in spite of the trauma He knew you would walk through. His plan for you includes all that He knows would happen in your lifetime, and yet His plan for you has always been good.

It doesn't matter who was not good to you or for you. When you partner with the Holy Spirit, He will align all things and weave all of your life experiences into a beautiful tapestry. He sees who you're becoming, not just who you've been. He knows what the world will gain when you're whole, not just what you'll personally experience.

You are worth the work.
Not because of what you've accomplished.
Not because of how strong you've been.
Simply because you are.

You are worth the work because you are fearfully and wonderfully made.
You are worth the work because God has plans for your life that require your wholeness to fulfill. You are worth the work because your healing creates space for others to believe in theirs. You are a worthy investment—not just for who you're becoming, but for who you've always been. God called you good from the beginning. He called you by name. He formed you with care, clothed you with purpose, and sealed you with worth.

In our culture, we often determine the worth of something by what someone is willing to pay for it. The rarer and the more precious, the higher the price. We see this with jewels, art, antiques... things deemed priceless because of their uniqueness and value.

And yet, when we reflect on our own worth, it's easy to forget just how valuable we are.

But God doesn't.

Jesus paid for your life with His own. With His blood. The spotless, sinless Lamb of God took on your shame, your pain, your guilt, and your story... because He believed you were worth it.

No price tag could ever capture the worth of the blood of Jesus.
It is sacred. It is priceless.
And that is what was given... for you.

So yes,
You are worth the work it takes to heal.
You are worth the energy it takes to grow.
You are worth the time it takes to walk in freedom.
You are worth the investment it takes to become whole.

If Jesus thought you were worth enduring the cross,
then you are most certainly worth the work of your healing journey.

You are not a problem to be fixed.

You are a treasure being uncovered.
Every step you take toward wholeness is a step of worship.
Every ounce of effort is evidence of faith.

You are worth the work.
Because you are loved.
Because you are chosen.
Because you are *His*.

Today's Focus

Today we're celebrating how far you've come while acknowledging the journey ahead. We're recognizing that your commitment to wholeness is valuable not just for you but for everyone whose life you touch. We're claiming your worth and declaring that the work is sacred.

DEEP REFLECTION QUESTIONS

Processing Your Worth and Vision for Wholeness

Take time to honestly examine your beliefs about your value and your vision for complete healing.

1. Your Worth Beliefs

Do you honestly believe you're worth the effort wholeness requires? Where do your beliefs about your worth come from?

....

....

....

....

2. Wholeness Vision

Describe your vision of wholeness. What would your life look like if you were completely whole—mind, body, and soul?

....

....

....

....

....

3. The Investment You've Made

Reflect on the work you've already invested in your healing. What efforts have you made that demonstrate your commitment to growth?

4. Gifts Under the Pain

What gifts, talents, or aspects of your personality have been buried under your pain? How might wholeness uncover these?

5. Your Ripple Effect

How has your healing journey already impacted others? How might your complete wholeness affect future generations?

Already impacted: ______________________

....

Future impact: ______________________

....

....

6. What You're Afraid to Lose

What are you afraid you might lose if you become completely whole? (Consider familiar identities, relationships, or ways of being that feel safe even if they're limiting)

....

....

....

....

7. Your Sacred Work

In what ways has your healing journey been an act of worship or service to God and others?

....

....

....

....

PERSONAL APPLICATION EXERCISES

Claiming Your Worth and Vision

Exercise 1: Worth Declaration

Complete these statements:

"I am worth the work of healing because..."

1.
2.
3.
4.
5.

"When I doubt my worth, I will remember that..."

"God's heart toward my healing is..."

Exercise 2: Wholeness Visualization

Physical Wholeness: What would complete physical health look like for you?

Emotional Wholeness: How would you handle emotions if you were completely healthy?

Relational Wholeness: What would your relationships look like if you were whole?

Spiritual Wholeness: How would your relationship with God be different?

Mental Wholeness: How would your thought patterns change?

Exercise 3: Legacy Planning

What I want to leave for the next generation: Instead of leaving _________________________________

I want to leave ______________________________

How my wholeness will impact my children/family:

....

....

....

What story I want my life to tell:

....

....

....

The cycle I'm breaking:

....

....

....

The new pattern I'm establishing:

....

....

....

WHOLENESS VISION WORKSHEETS

Creating Your Wholeness Blueprint

Your Whole Life Vision
In 5 years, when I'm walking in wholeness:

My relationship with myself will be:

....

....

....

My relationship with God will be:

....

....

....

My family relationships will be:

....

....

....

My friendships will be:

....

....

My work/calling will be:

....

....

....

My physical health will be:

....

....

....

My emotional capacity will be:

....

....

....

How I'll spend my time:

....

....

....

The impact I'll have:

....

....

Bridging the Gap

Where I am now vs. Where I'm going:

Current Reality: _______________________

....

Wholeness Vision: _______________________

....

The gap between them: _______________________

....

Steps needed to bridge this gap:

1.
3.
4.
5.
6.

Your Wholeness Commitment

I commit to pursuing wholeness because:

....

....

....

I will not settle for:

....

....

....

I will pursue:

....

....

....

When I'm tempted to quit, I will remember:

....

....

....

My accountability for this commitment:

Who: _______________________________

How: _______________________________

When: _______________________________

Celebrating Progress

How far I've come since beginning this journey:

....

....

....

Evidence that God is working in my healing:

....

....

....

What I'm most proud of:

....

....

....

How I want to celebrate my progress:

....

....

....

ACTION PLANNING & PRAYER

Your Day 5 Commitments

Moving Forward in Wholeness, I Will:

Choose 2-3 specific commitments that honor your worth and vision:

1. ____

Why this matters for my wholeness: _________________ Timeline: _______________________

2. ____

Why this matters for my wholeness: _________________ Timeline: _______________________

3. ____

Why this matters for my wholeness: _________________ Timeline: _______________________

Your Worth Reminder System

When I doubt my worth, I will:

- ☐ Reread my worth declarations from today
- ☐ Call my accountability partner
- ☐ Read Scripture about my identity in Christ
- ☐ Look at evidence of progress I've made
- ☐ Remember the people my healing will impact
- ☐ Other: _______________________________

Daily worth affirmation I'll speak:

"I am worth the work of healing because ____."

Legacy Planning

One pattern I commit to breaking in my family line:

....

One new pattern I commit to establishing:

....

How I'll model wholeness for others:

....

....

Long-term Vision Accountability

Who I'll share my wholeness vision with:

....

....

How they can support my long-term journey:

....

....

When we'll check in on my progress:

....

....

Support for the Journey Ahead

Resources I need for continued healing:

....

....

Professional support I'll maintain or seek:

....

....

Community connections I'll nurture:

....

....

Prayer for Wholeness Worth

Heavenly Father,

Thank You for seeing me as worth the investment of wholeness. When I'm tempted to settle for partial healing or believe I don't deserve complete restoration, remind me of Your heart toward me.

Help me see my healing journey as sacred work that honors You and serves others. Give me vision for who I'm becoming and patience with the process of getting there.

Show me the gifts You've placed in me that are waiting to be uncovered through wholeness. Help me believe that my complete healing will create space for others to believe in theirs.

I commit to not settling for survival when You've called me to thrive. Give me courage to pursue complete wholeness in mind, body, and soul.

Use my healing to break generational cycles and establish new patterns of health for those who come after me.

I declare that I am worth the work because You say I am.

In Jesus' name, amen.

Personal Prayer Space

Write your own prayer about your worth and commitment to wholeness:

....

....

....

....

....

....

....

....

Wholeness Declaration

"I am worth the work of complete healing. I will not settle for _____________________

when God has called me to _______________. My wholeness matters because _________________."

When will you speak this declaration daily?

....

....

....

....

ADDITIONAL REFLECTION SPACE

Additional Insights and Processing

Use this space for continued reflection on your worth, your vision for wholeness, and any insights that emerged during today's work. You might also want to process any emotions that came up around claiming your value.

Celebrating Your Sacred Work

The most meaningful insight from these 5 phases:

....

....

....

How my view of healing has changed:

....

....

....

Evidence that this work has been worth it:

....

....

....

What I'm most grateful for in this journey:

....

....

....

....

Continuing the Journey

The most important thing I learned about myself:

....

....

....

The most important thing I learned about God:

....

....

....

How I'll continue pursuing wholeness:

....

....

....

My biggest commitment moving forward:

....

....

....

....

"For I know the plans I have for you," declares the Lord, "plans to prosper you and not to harm you, to give you hope and a future." — Jeremiah 29:11 (NIV)

You have chosen to believe that your wholeness is worth the work. You have declared your value and committed to the sacred journey of complete healing. God's plans for your prosperity include wholeness in every area of your life. You are worth every effort this journey requires.

ONGOING SUPPORT MATERIALS

MY TESTIMONY - WHEN GOD RESTORES
WHAT WAS BROKEN

My Physical Healing: From Death's Door to Divine Restoration

In 2021, I experienced what can only be described as a divine intervention disguised as a medical crisis. After taking an antibiotic called Bactrim, my immune system turned on me. My platelets dropped to dangerously low levels due to a rare autoimmune condition called Immune Thrombocytopenia (ITP).

When I arrived at the emergency room, my platelet count was 10,000. By the time I was admitted, it had plummeted to just 3,000. To put that into perspective, a healthy range is between 200,000 and 400,000. I was bleeding internally — blood blisters formed in my mouth; petechiae covered my skin, and I was at serious risk of hemorrhaging.

I was hospitalized immediately, placed on strict bed rest, and given two platelet transfusions along with intravenous immunoglobulin (IVIG). Even basic activities like brushing my teeth or shifting in bed became dangerous. My body was in crisis, and I was terrified.

But that acute emergency was only the tip of the iceberg.

For years leading up to that moment, I had been battling chronic health issues: severe anemia, frequent diverticulitis flare-ups, intestinal malabsorption, and crushing fatigue. From 2018 to 2021, I endured repeated flare-ups of diverticulitis, never realizing these were warning signs of something deeper. Despite trying supplements, dietary changes, and IV infusions, nothing seemed to truly restore me.

I now understand that this wasn't just a physical issue; it was the result of **years of unprocessed, internalized stress** that had worn down my immune system and ravaged my gut. I had been living in survival mode for so long, pushing through exhaustion, pain, and emotional weight, that my body eventually broke down under the pressure. I wasn't managing my stress; I was suppressing it. And it was costing me everything.

I had resigned myself to a life of symptom management. I believed healing was out of reach. But then, in December 2024, something shifted.

A friend introduced me to a line of nutraceuticals. At first, I was curious because of their GLP-1 benefits for weight management. But what I received was far greater than weight loss — I received the beginning of physical restoration.

Within weeks, my energy started to return, and my mind felt clearer. I didn't realize how numb I'd been until I began to feel again. And then came the real confirmation: at my 2025 hematologist appointment, my bloodwork was the best it had been since my ITP diagnosis. My quarterly visits were reduced to annual checkups. My platelets were stable. My body was healing.

While I still carry the diagnosis of ITP, it no longer carries me. My life is no longer ruled by fear, fatigue, or flare-ups. I feel amazing — energized, restored, and more aligned with my purpose than ever before.

What began as a search for something to help me feel better on the outside became a gateway to deep, lasting healing on the inside.

God used my pursuit of physical wellness to restore far more than my body — He restored my confidence, reconnected me with community, and reignited my sense of purpose.

My Emotional Healing: The Restoration That Made Everything Else possible

My healing journey didn't begin with a doctor's visit or a diagnosis. It began inside of me.

For years, I carried invisible wounds, deep emotional scars shaped by childhood experiences and further reinforced by a long-term, on-again off-again relationship in my young adulthood that spanned nearly two decades. That relationship, though complicated and deeply woven into my life, became both a mirror of my unhealed pain and a breeding ground for cycles of emotional, verbal, and at times, physical harm.

It was a connection I could never fully sever, even after I chose to close the door emotionally. Its lasting ties made the healing even more layered. But in 2022, I found the courage to step away from the version of myself that relationship had defined — the one who stayed silent, diminished, and disconnected from her worth.

That single act of emotional bravery became the turning point. It was the moment I stopped surviving and started healing.

Closing that chapter wasn't just about relational boundaries; it was about internal liberation. It marked the beginning of a season of radical self-love and spiritual restoration. And as I surrendered that relationship, something began to shift in every other area of my life, especially in my body.

Because what I now understand is this: **my physical healing couldn't fully begin until I addressed the emotional wounds that were silently draining me from the inside out.**

For years, chronic stress had been attacking my immune system, disrupting my gut health, and weakening my body. But the stress wasn't just circumstantial; it was stored in my nervous system, locked in my cells, and rooted in unhealed emotional pain. When I finally began releasing the weight of that pain, my body could finally begin to recover.

As God healed my heart, He began to heal my health. The more I released, the more I received. The more I forgave, the more I flourished. The more I told the truth — even when it hurt — the more whole I became.

He rebuilt me from the inside out, layer by layer, lie by lie, phase by phase. Just like the moon, my healing was not linear. Some phases were bright and full. Others felt hidden and quiet. But even in the darkness, His light in me never stopped shining.

He restored my identity.
He restored my voice.
He restored the truth of who I am.
And as He rebuilt me emotionally, He strengthened me physically.

My confidence returned.
My capacity to love expanded.
My desire to show up for others increased.
My hope was reignited.

My Healing Journey Extends Far Beyond the Physical

The invisible wounds of my soul often cut the deepest, and mine were carved by years of physical, verbal, and emotional abuse. I carried scars from heartbreak, shame that whispered lies about my worth, and a deep-seated belief that I was fundamentally not enough.

That sense of unworthiness became the soundtrack of my life for years. It influenced every relationship, every decision, every dream I dared to have or abandon. I lived as though I had to constantly prove my right to take up space in the world.

But God is in the business of restoration. Slowly, patiently, lovingly, He began healing the broken pieces of my heart. He started stripping away the lies I had believed about myself

and rebuilding my identity with His truth. Like Joel 2:25 promises, He began restoring what had been stolen from me — piece by precious piece.

The process wasn't quick or easy. It required facing memories I had buried, feeling emotions I had numbed, and challenging thought patterns that had become second nature. But with each layer of healing, I discovered more of who I really was beneath the pain.

Today, I walk in a freedom I once thought was impossible. The shame that once defined me has been replaced with an unshakeable worth. The guilt that followed me like a shadow has been swallowed up by grace. I no longer exhaust myself trying to prove my value — I rest in knowing I already have it.

🕊 My Village Walked with Me — Then and Now

I am profoundly grateful to my village, the family and friends who walked with me through every valley and celebrated with me on every mountaintop. Their love became my lifeline during the seasons when I couldn't see past my pain. Every phone call that interrupted my isolation, every text message that reminded me I wasn't forgotten, every act of love (both grand and seemingly small) were threads that God used to weave strength back into my spirit.

They didn't just stand by and watch my struggle; they stepped into it with me. When I couldn't find the words to pray, they prayed for me. When I couldn't see my own worth, they held up mirrors of truth and showed me who I really was beneath the pain. They loved me through the hard days, the lonely nights, and the moments when my faith felt too fragile to hold. They helped me discover an inner strength; I never knew existed, not because they gave it to me, but because they believed in it so fiercely that I began to believe in it too.

And they still show up for me.

They continue to pray, encourage, and hold space for me when life grows heavy. Their presence reminds me that God often sends healing through people — and I am blessed to have been surrounded by a village who never let me forget who I was, even when I had forgotten myself.

My two sons became my anchor and my inspiration.

In their eyes, I see the woman I'm fighting to become. Their presence reminds me that this battle isn't just about my own healing; it's about breaking cycles, modeling resilience, and leaving them a legacy of wholeness rather than wounds. I want to continue breaking cycles so they won't have to survive them. Their need for a whole mother was and remains to be my fuel when my own tank feels empty.

🏆 I Am Living Proof

Today, I stand healed — not perfect, not finished, but whole.
Whole in identity.

Whole in truth.
Whole in worth.
And whole in the God who makes all things new.

I am loved.
I am chosen.
I am worthy.
And I am walking out healing every single day.

If you are reading this and wondering whether healing is possible for you, let my life be your answer. God restores what pain tries to destroy. God illuminates what shame tries to hide. God rebuilds what trauma tries to tear down.

He has done it and continues to do it for me — and He will also do it for you.

PRACTICAL STEPS TO WALK OUT YOUR HEALING

Healing touches your spirit, soul (mind, will, emotions), and body. While God does the heavy lifting, He invites us to participate through intentional choices and daily habits. Here are thirty practical ways to cooperate with His healing work in your life:

Spirit-Focused Practices (1-6)

1. **Start each day with Scripture** - Let God's Word be the first voice you hear each morning
2. **End each day with gratitude** - Write down three things you're thankful for before bed
3. **Pray through your feelings** - Don't just pray about circumstances; pray about emotions
4. **Worship when you don't feel like it** - Sometimes praise unlocks breakthrough
5. **Fast for clarity** - Consider fasting from food, social media, or distractions to hear God
6. **Practice spiritual disciplines** - Engage regularly in prayer, Bible reading, and meditation

Mind Renewal Practices (7-12)

7. **Journal your truth** - Write honestly about your feelings without censoring yourself
8. **Challenge negative thoughts** - Question lies and replace them with God's truth
9. **Read encouraging content** - Feed your mind with hope, truth, and inspiration
10. **Limit negative media** - Protect your mental space from toxic information
11. **Practice mindfulness** - Learn to be present with thoughts and feelings without judgment
12. **Seek counseling** - Professional therapy is holy ground when God is in it

Will and Decision-Making Practices (13-18)

13. **Set healthy boundaries** - Learn to say no to what drains you and yes to what fills you
14. **Make values-based choices** - Align decisions with your principles, not fears
15. **End toxic relationships** - Some people are meant to be loved from a distance
16. **Choose forgiveness daily** - Forgiveness is not about them; it's about your freedom
17. **Take responsibility** - Own your choices without taking blame for others' actions
18. **Follow through on commitments** - Build trust with yourself through consistent action

Emotional Health Practices (19-24)

19. **Feel your feelings fully** - Allow yourself to experience emotions without immediately fixing them
20. **Practice self-compassion** - Speak to yourself with kindness, not criticism

21. **Celebrate small wins** - Acknowledge progress, even when it feels insignificant
22. **Build supportive relationships** - Surround yourself with people who celebrate your growth
23. **Express emotions creatively** - Use art, music, writing, or movement to process feelings
24. **Join a support group** - Connect with others on similar healing journeys

Physical Health Practices (25-30)

25. **Move your body daily** - Even a short walk can shift energy and improve mood
26. **Prioritize sleep** - Your body and mind heal during rest; make it non-negotiable
27. **Eat to fuel healing** - Choose foods that nourish rather than just fill
28. **Stay hydrated** - Dehydration affects both physical and mental clarity
29. **Take healing baths** - Use this time to wash away stress and reset your spirit
30. **Consider medical support** - Sometimes brain chemistry needs professional intervention

Remember: You don't have to implement all thirty at once. Choose one or two that resonate most with you right now and build from there. Small, consistent steps create lasting transformation.

WEEKLY CHECK-IN TEMPLATE

Use this template each week to maintain momentum in your healing journey. Copy this format into your journal or notebook.

Date: _______________

This Week's Reflection

1. How are you doing with your healing commitments from the 5-day journey? Scale of 1-10: ___

....

....

....

2. What challenges or obstacles did you face this week?

....

....

....

3. What victories—big or small—can you celebrate?

....

....

....

4. Where do you sense God working in your healing?

....

....

....

5. What emotions have been most present this week?

....

....

....

How did you handle them?

....

....

....

Mind, Will, and Emotions Check

Mind (Thoughts and Beliefs): What thoughts have been challenging this week? _______________

....

What truths do you need to focus on? _______________

....

Will (Choices and Decisions): What healthy choices did you make? _______________

....

What decisions do you need to make moving forward? _______________

....

Emotions (Feelings and Responses): What emotions felt overwhelming? _______________

....

How can you better care for your emotional health? _______

Next Week's Focus

One thing I want to continue:

One thing I want to improve:

One new practice I want to try:

Prayer focus for next week:

Accountability check-in scheduled with: _____________ **Date/Time:** ______________________

MONTHLY PROGRESS REVIEW

Complete this assessment monthly to track your longer-term healing journey.

Month/Year: _______________

Growth Assessment

Rate each area from 1-10 (1 = significant struggle, 10 = healthy and whole):

Emotional Health: ___/10 *(Last month: ___)*
Self-Worth: ___/10 *(Last month: ___)*
Past Trauma Impact: ___/10 *(Last month: ___)*
Forgiveness (Others): ___/10 *(Last month: ___)*
Forgiveness (Self): ___/10 *(Last month: ___)*
Spiritual Health: ___/10 *(Last month: ___)*
Physical Health: ___/10 *(Last month: ___)*
Relationships: ___/10 *(Last month: ___)*
Boundaries: ___/10 *(Last month: ___)*
Life Purpose: ___/10 *(Last month: ___)*

Progress Reflection

Biggest breakthrough this month:

....

....

....

Most challenging area:

....

....

....

How you've grown:

....

....

What you've learned about God:

....

....

What you've learned about yourself:

....

....

Looking Forward

Top 3 priorities for next month:

1.
2.
3.

Support I need:

....

....

One way I'll celebrate my progress:

....

....

DIFFICULT DAYS TOOLKIT

Some days will be harder than others. Use these tools during challenging times.

When You Feel Overwhelmed

Immediate Steps:

1. Take 5 deep breaths
2. Name 3 things you can see, 2 you can hear, 1 you can touch
3. Remind yourself: "This feeling will pass"
4. Do one small self-care action

Grounding Questions:

- What do I need right now?
- What small step can I take?
- Who can I reach out to for support?
- What truth do I need to remember?

When Progress Feels Slow

Remember:

- Healing happens in layers, not linear progression
- Small steps count more than dramatic breakthroughs
- God is working even when you can't see evidence
- Your timeline doesn't have to match anyone else's

Action Steps:

- Review your progress from last month
- Celebrate one small victory from this week
- Adjust expectations to be more realistic
- Focus on process rather than outcomes

When You Want to Give Up

Read This: You are not behind in your healing. You are exactly where you need to be. The work you're doing matters. The effort you're making is seen and valued. You are worth every bit of energy this journey requires.

Emergency Contacts:

- National Suicide Prevention Lifeline: 988
- Crisis Text Line: Text HOME to 741741
- Your therapist: _______________________
- Trusted friend: _______________________
- Pastor/spiritual advisor: _______________

When You Have a Setback

Reframe It:

- Setbacks are part of the process, not evidence of failure
- Every step backward teaches you something valuable
- Healing isn't about perfection; it's about persistence
- God's grace covers your difficult days

Recovery Plan:

1. Be compassionate with yourself
2. Identify what triggered the setback
3. Adjust your approach based on what you learned
4. Reach out for additional support if needed
5. Take the next small step forward

Daily Reminder

"And we know that in all things God works for the good of those who love him, who have been called according to his purpose." — Romans 8:28 (NIV)

Even your difficult days are part of God's healing work in your life.

CELEBRATION & BREAKTHROUGH PAGES

Breakthrough Moments

Document your victories, breakthroughs, and moments of hope.

Date: _____________ **Breakthrough:** _________________________

....

How it felt: _________________________

....

Date: _____________ **Breakthrough:** _________________________

....

How it felt: _________________________

....

Date: _____________ **Breakthrough:** _________________________

....

How it felt: _________________________

....

Physical Health Improvements:

....

....

Emotional Growth:

....

....

Relationship Changes:

....

....

Spiritual Development:

....

....

New Boundaries Set:

....

....

Patterns Broken:

....

....

People Who Have Supported Your Healing

Name: ___________________ How they helped: ___________________________________

Name: ___________________ How they helped: ___________________________________

Name: ___________________ How they helped: ___________________________________

Gratitude List for Your Healing Journey

1.
2.
3.
4.
5.
6.
7.
8.
9.
10.

Evidence of God's Faithfulness

Ways God has shown up in your healing:

Prayers He has answered:

....

....

....

....

....

Unexpected gifts in the process:

....

....

....

....

....

A LETTER OF HOPE

Dear Beautiful Soul,

If you've made it to this page, you've already taken the most important step: you've decided to begin. In a world that often tells us to push through, ignore our pain, or pretend everything is fine, you've chosen something radical—you've chosen healing.

I want you to know something that I wish someone had told me at the beginning of my journey: you are worth the work. You are worth the work of healing, no matter how long the road stretches before you, no matter how many tears you shed, no matter how many times you have to start again.

There is nothing—absolutely nothing—you will regret about doing the hard work of healing. Not one moment of honest reflection, not one difficult conversation, not one boundary you set, not one journal entry you write. It's all part of the walk, and it's all working together for your good.

The road may be longer than you hoped. There may be setbacks that discourage you and seasons that test your resolve. You may have days when you wonder if healing is really possible or if you have what it takes to keep going. On those days, remember this: God is not finished with your story. The same power that raised Jesus from the dead is at work in you, bringing life to places that felt permanently dead.

Your healing matters—not just to you, but to everyone whose life you will touch. When you break generational cycles, you set future generations free. When you choose wholeness over hiding, you give others permission to do the same. When you refuse to settle for surviving and insist on thriving, you become a living testament to God's faithfulness.

Take your time. Rest when you need to. Ask for help when you're struggling. But please, don't give up. The world needs what you carry, but it can only receive it when you're whole enough to offer it from a place of overflow rather than deficit.

You are loved beyond measure. You are seen in your struggle. You are held in your healing. And you are worth every bit of effort this journey requires.

Walk it out, beautiful one. Walk it out with Him.

With love and hope for your journey,

Marie-Renée

"And we know that in all things God works for the good of those who love him, who have been called according to his purpose." — Romans 8:28 (NIV)

ADDITIONAL RESOURCES & CONNECT WITH MARIE-RENÉE

Recommended Reading

For Emotional Healing:

- *Boundaries* by Henry Cloud and John Townsend
- *It's Not Supposed to Be This Way* by Lysa TerKeurst
- *Good Boundaries and Goodbyes* by Lysa TerKeurst
- *The Self Care Prescription* by Robin L. Gobin, Ph.D
- *Set Boundaries, Find Peace* by Nedra Glover Tawwab

For Spiritual Growth:

- *Battlefield of the Mind* by Joyce Meyer
- *Present Over Perfect* by Shauna Niequist
- *Your Story Has a Villain* by Jonathan "JP" Pokluda

Scripture References for Healing

- **Isaiah 61:1-3** (Beauty for ashes)
- **Romans 8:28** (All things work together for good)
- **2 Corinthians 5:17** (New creation)
- **Joel 2:25** (Restoration of what was stolen)
- **Jeremiah 30:17** (God will restore your health)
- **Psalm 147:3** (He heals the brokenhearted)
- **Philippians 4:13** (I can do all things through Christ)
- **Matthew 11:28-30** (Come to me, all who are weary)

Crisis Support

If you're experiencing thoughts of self-harm:

- **National Suicide Prevention Lifeline:** 988
- **Crisis Text Line:** Text HOME to 741741
- **Your local emergency services:** 911

Professional Help Resources

- **Psychology Today:** psychologytoday.com (therapist directory)
- **Your insurance provider's website** for covered therapists
- **Local churches** often have counseling ministries
- **Community mental health centers** offer sliding scale fees

Remember: Seeking professional help is a sign of strength, not weakness.

Connect with Marie-Renée

Wellness Products: The nutraceuticals that supported my physical healing journey: **MarieNorman.threeinternational.com**

Clean Beauty: Nourish your body from the outside in with clean beauty products: www.counter.com/?aff=MARIENORMAN

Follow the Journey: Instagram: @holisticallyher.marie **TikTok:** @reberee

A Final Word

Remember: True healing touches every part of you—spirit, soul (mind, will, emotions), and body. These resources support your journey toward complete wholeness.

Your healing journey is sacred. Every page you've completed in this workbook is evidence of your courage and commitment to becoming whole. Keep walking it out.

"He has sent me to bind up the brokenhearted, to proclaim freedom for the captives and release from darkness for the prisoners." — Isaiah 61:1 (NIV)